I am not a girl or a boy.

I am just an it.

If I get inside you, I can make you sick.

You may know me as Covid or the Flu.

I don't care who I choose,

So be careful it's not you.

Don't be scared.

Don't be scared.

There are things you can do,
to keep Vinny the Virus away
from you.

Some are good. Most are bad.

Many of them can make you very sad.

They are very
small and are not alive.

In the cells of humans,
animals, plants,
bacteria and
fungi they hide.

There are 10 viruses in and around
the tree.

Can you find them?

They hijack your cells as an uninvited guest, but it is their only way to survive.

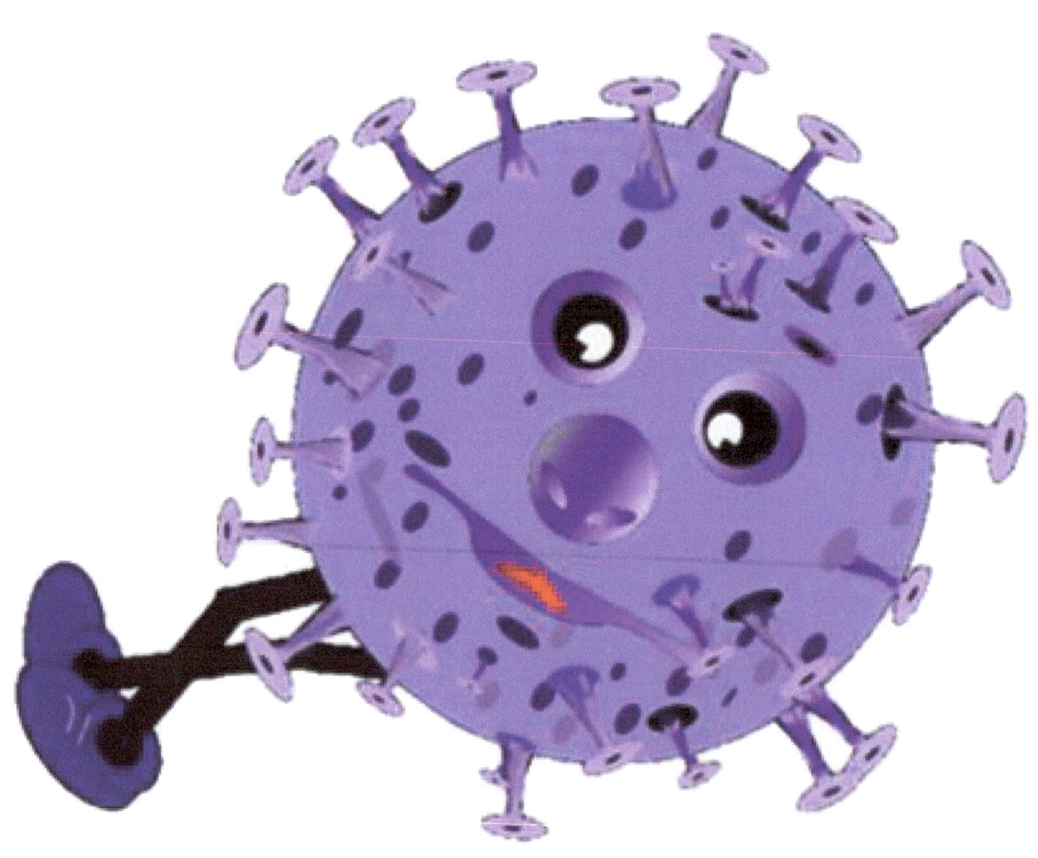

They multiply in the hundreds and hundreds.

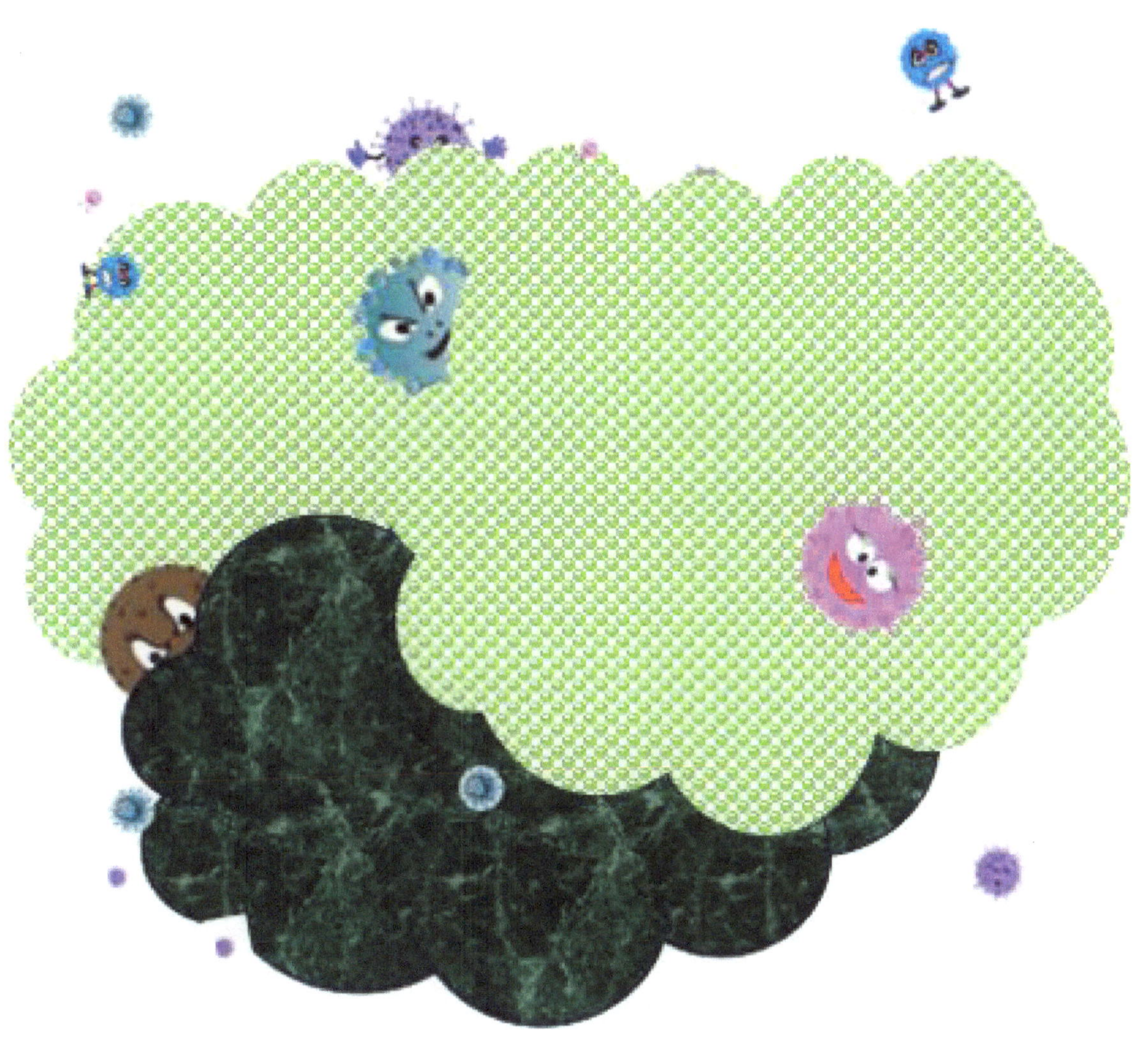

They soon become thousands and thousands.

Then millions and millions.

That is when you can become very sick.

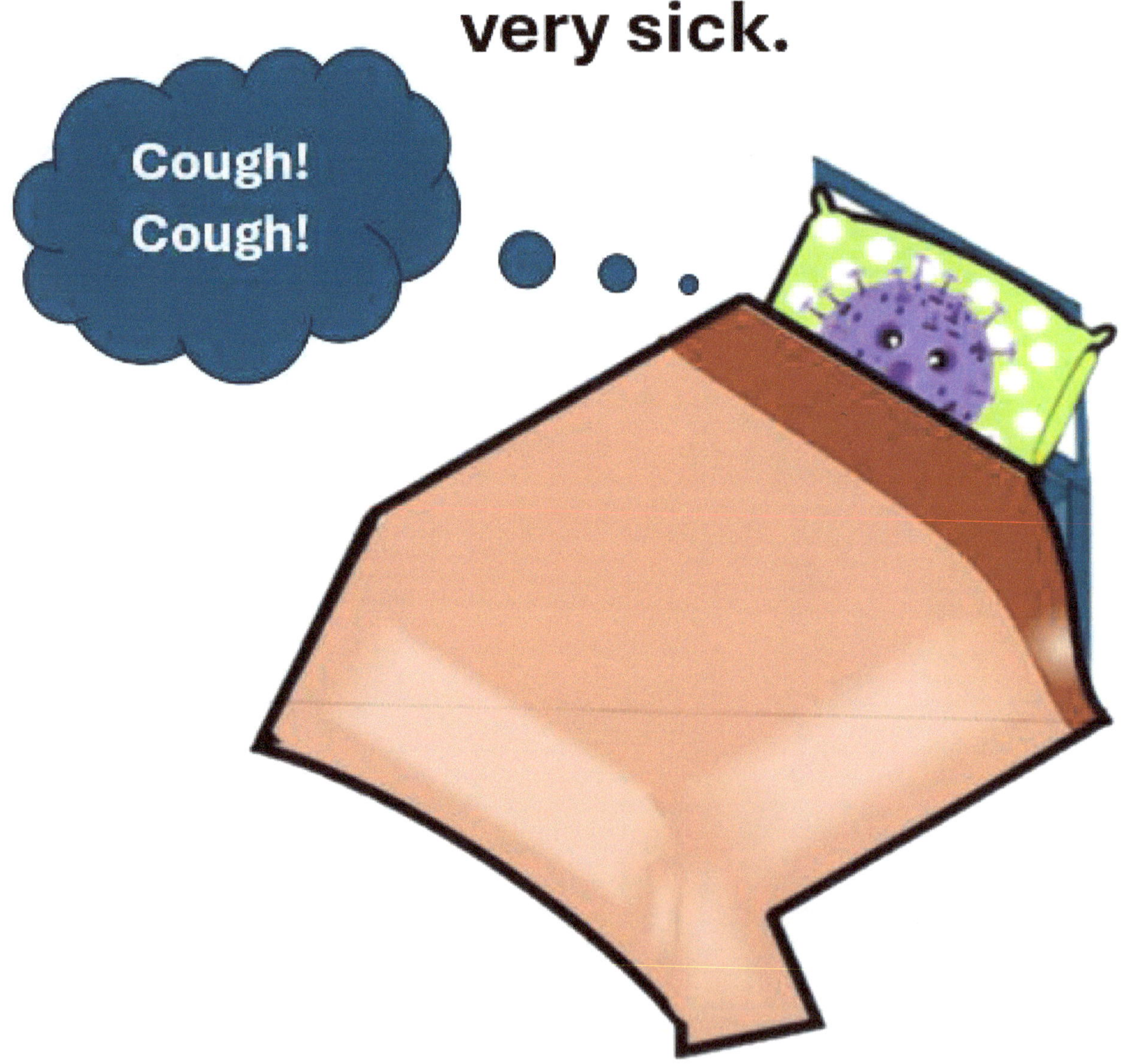

Don't be scared.

Don't be scared.

There are things you can do, to keep Vinny the Virus away from you.

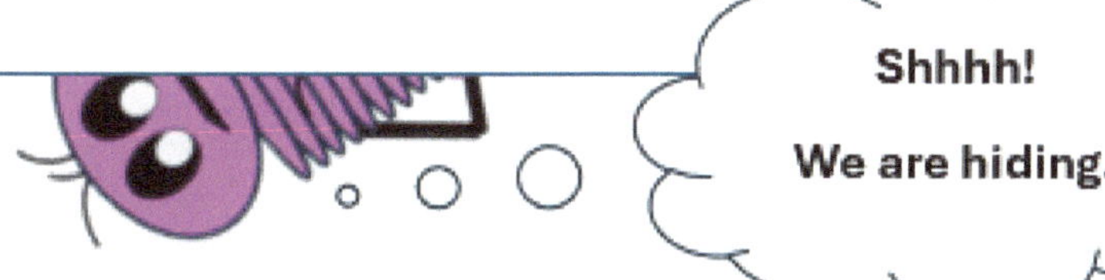

We come in many shapes and forms.

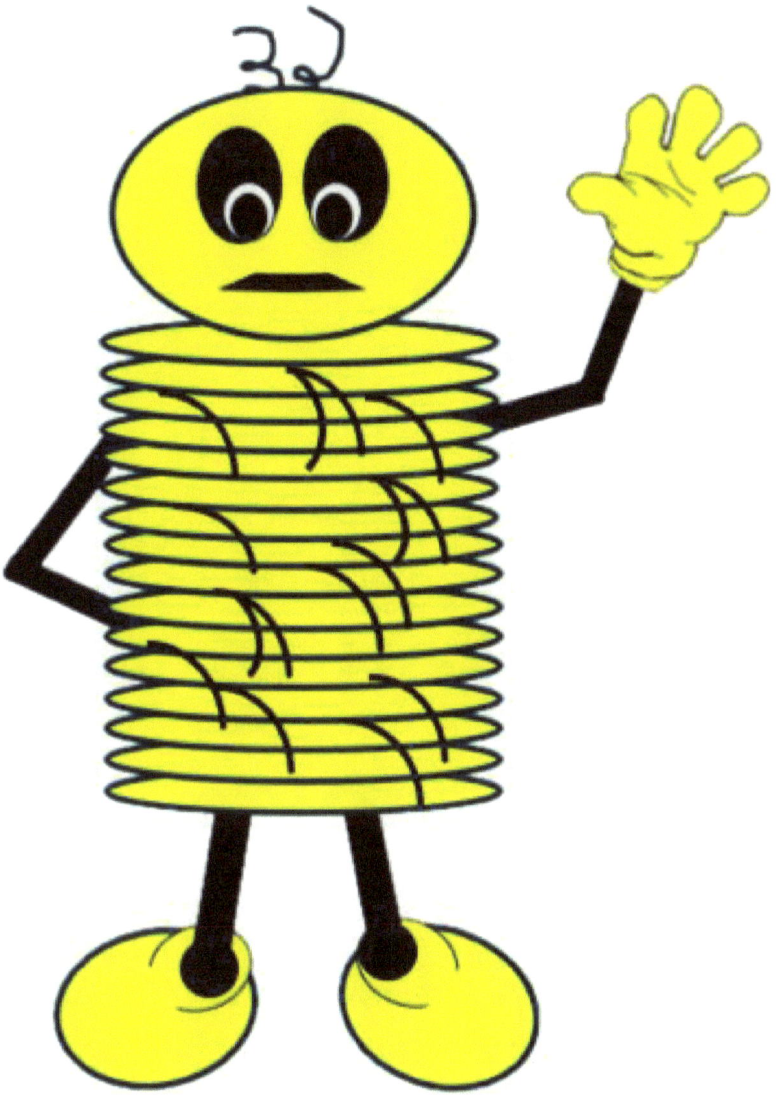

I look like a tube and can tall or small.

I'm an Envelope (En-ve-lope) Virus.
I am round and look like a ball.

I am a geometric shape with 20 sides.

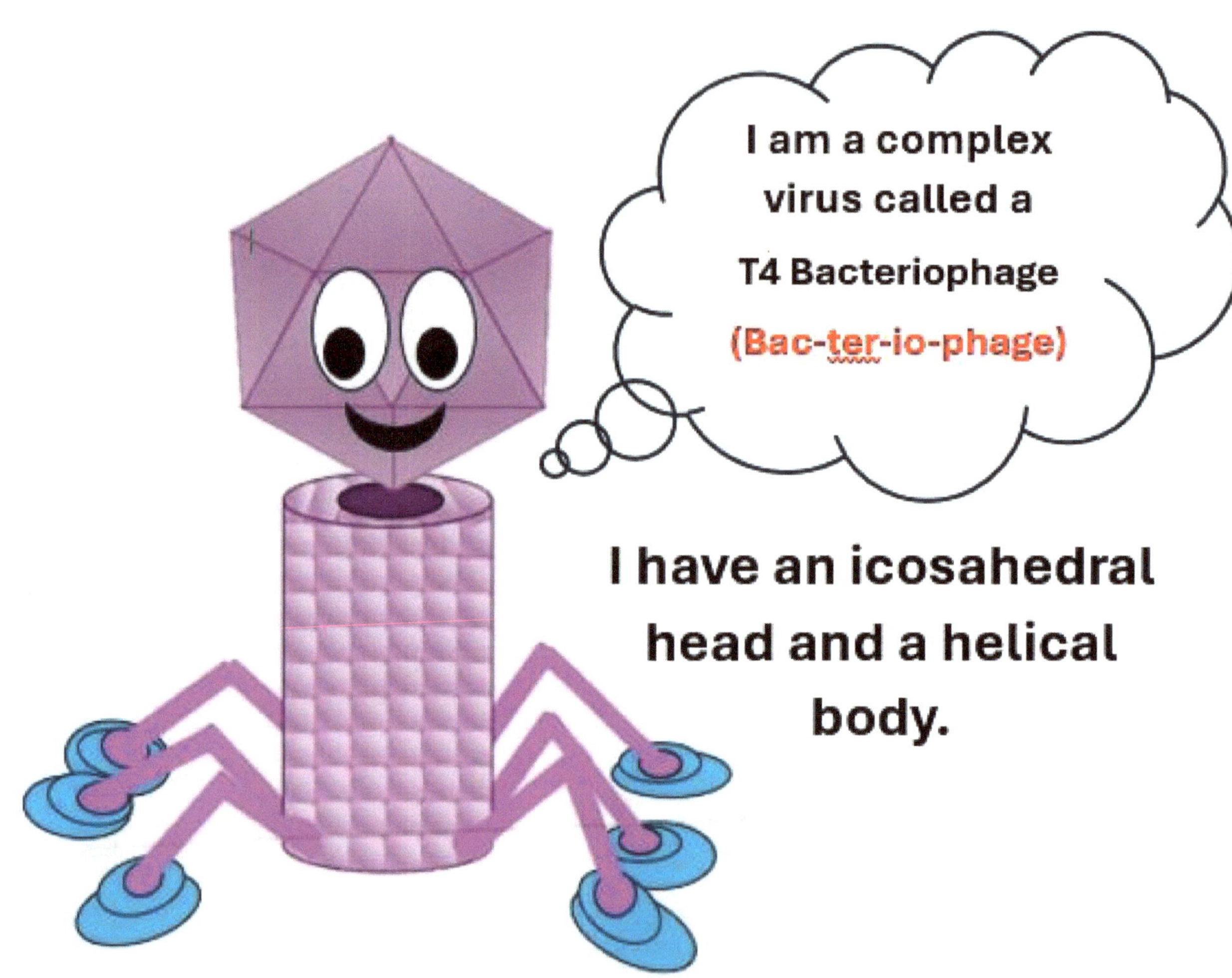

I am a complex virus called a T4 Bacteriophage
(Bac-ter-io-phage)
I have an icosahedral head and a helical body.
I also have structures that look like legs.

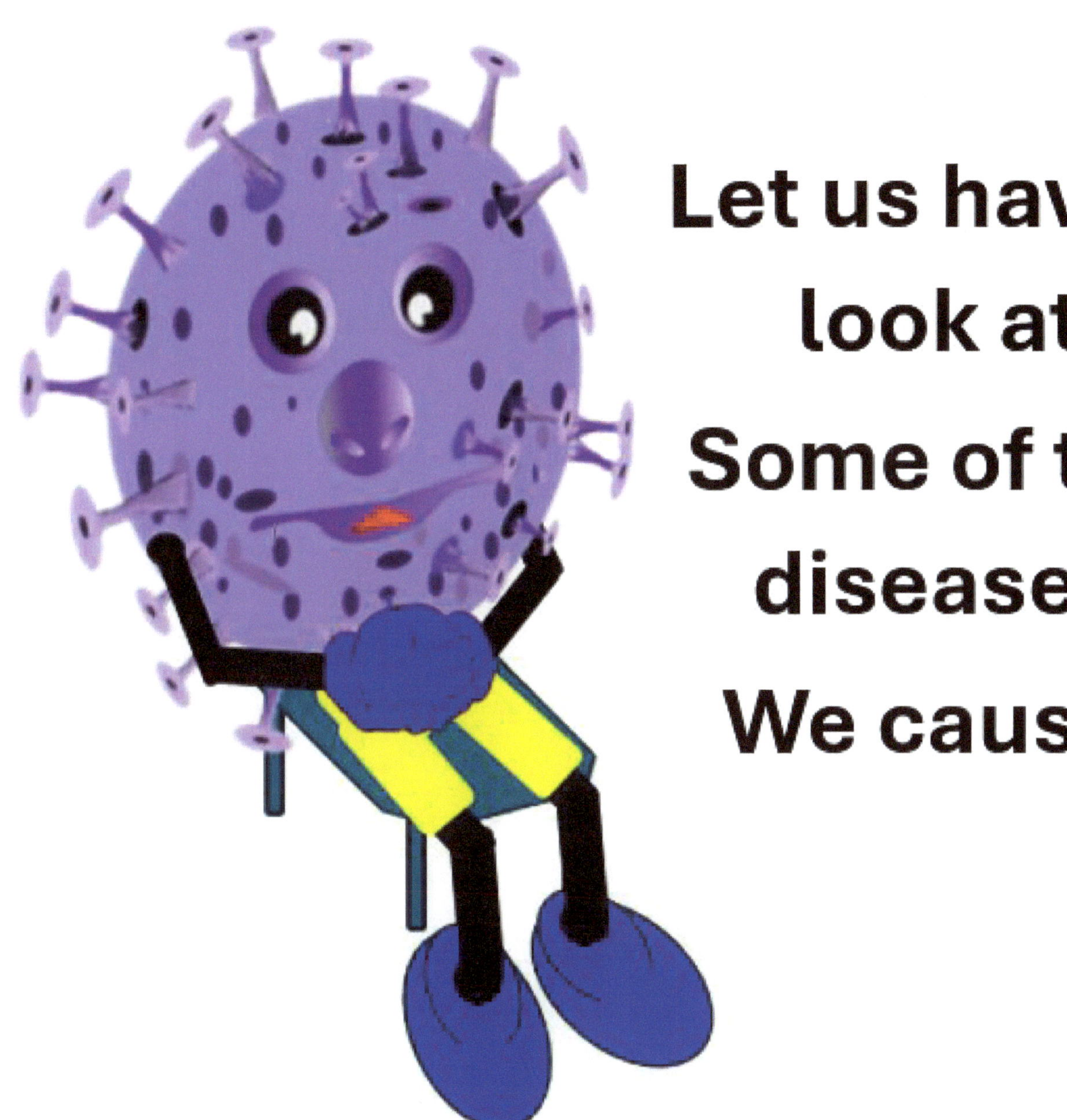

Let us have a
look at
Some of the
diseases
We cause.

Envelope Virus

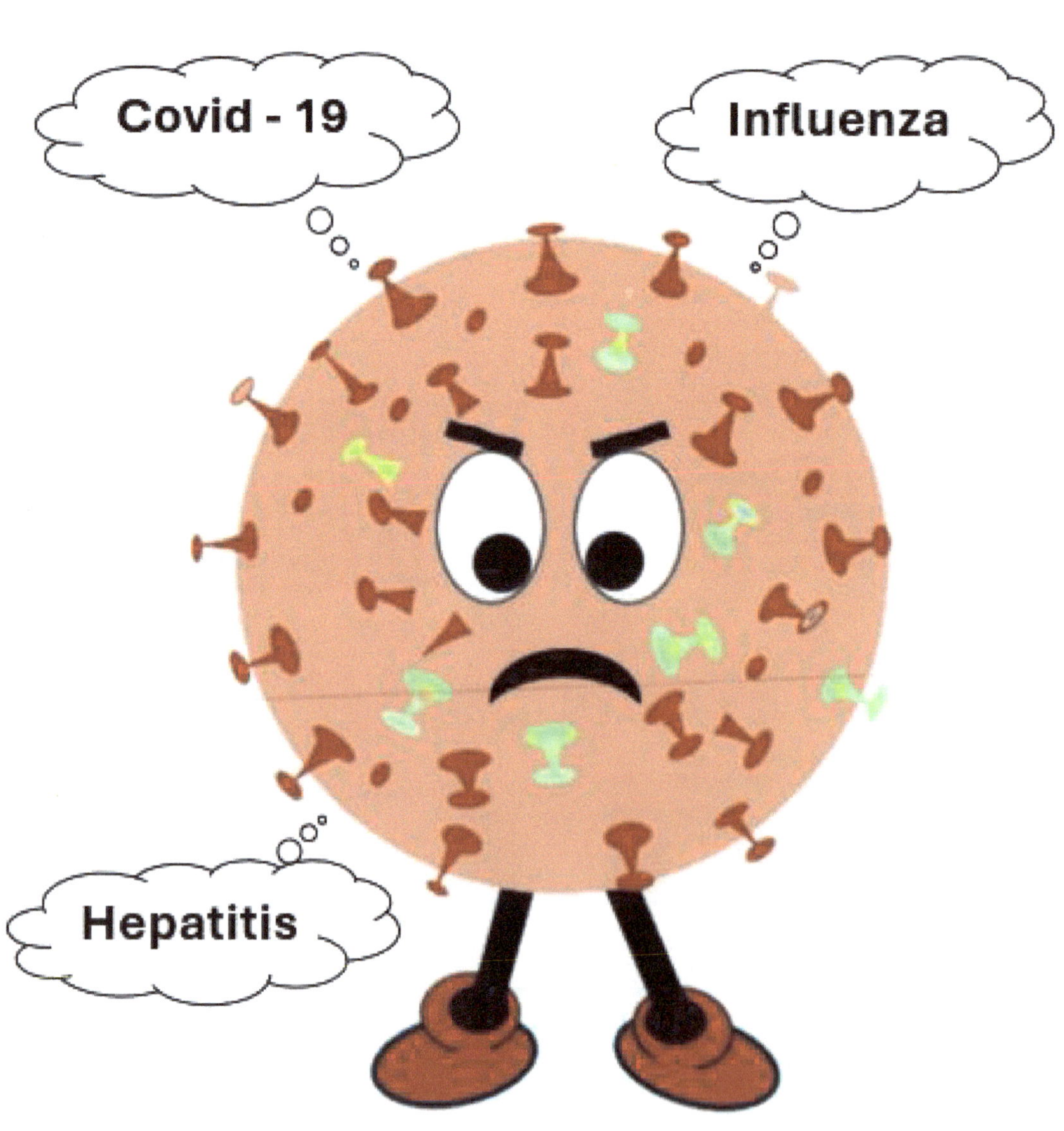

T4 Bacteriophage

Although I have

a different name,

I am a virus all the

same.

I affect viruses and

will not harm you.

Icosahedral Virus

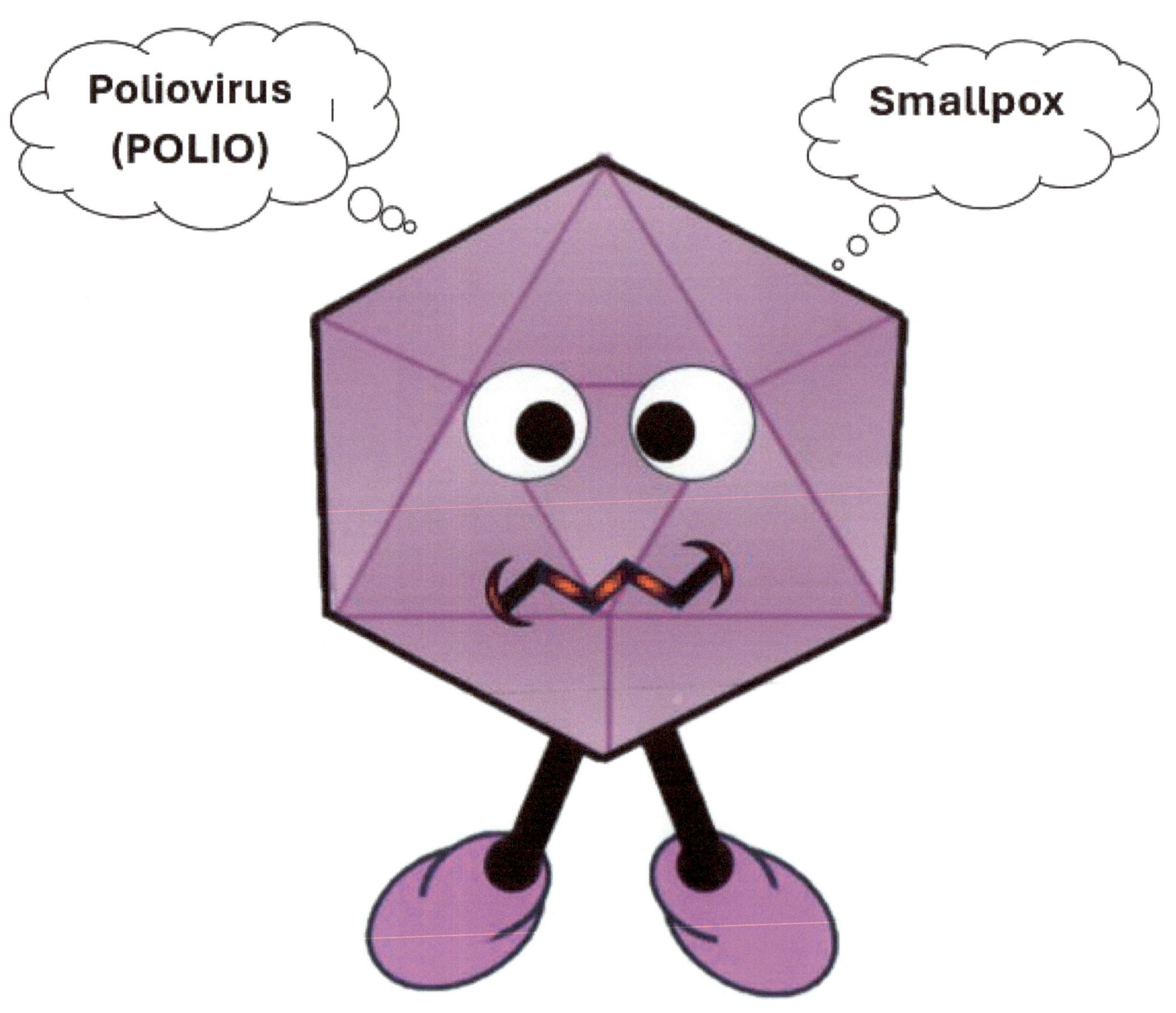

Helical Virus

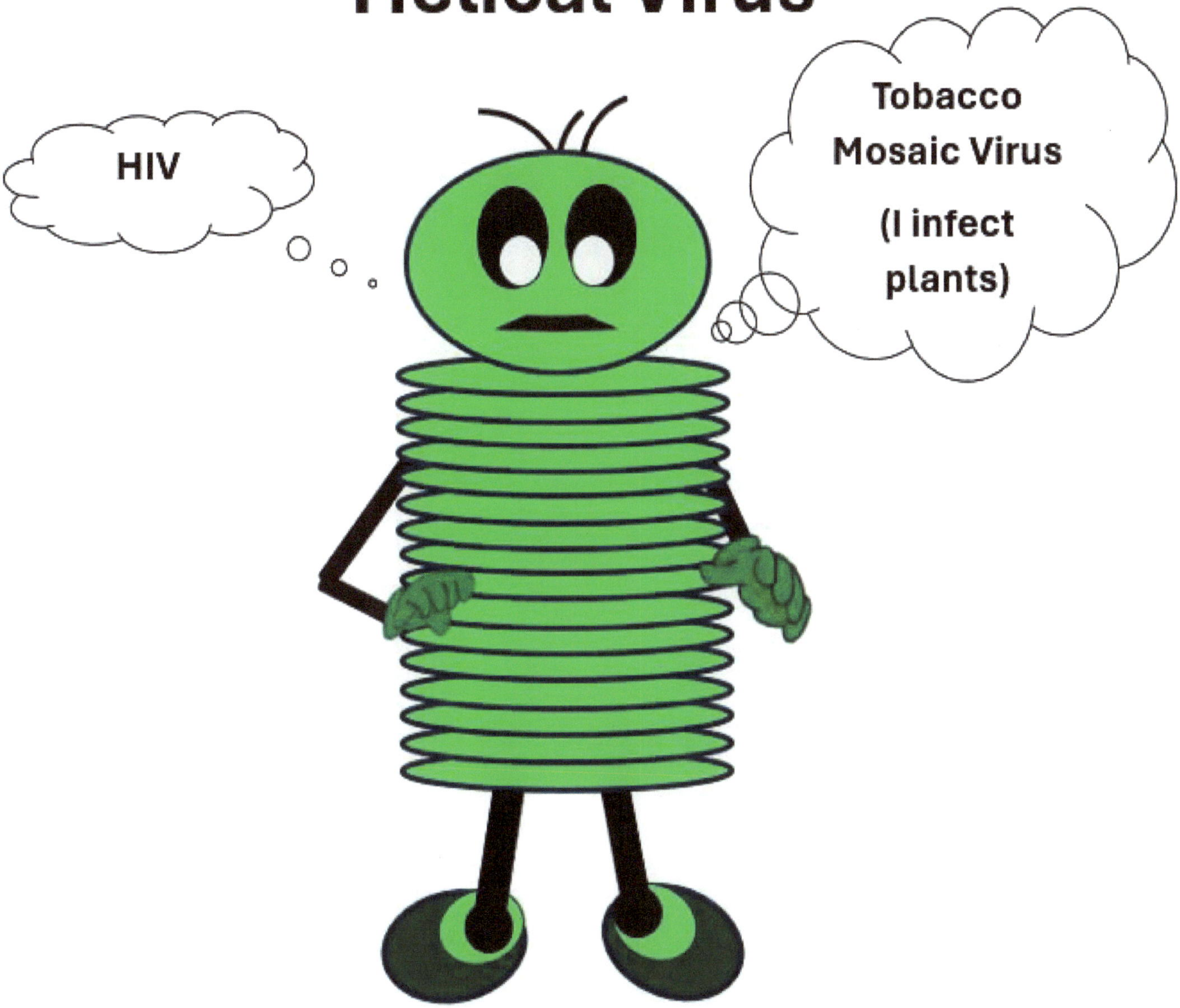

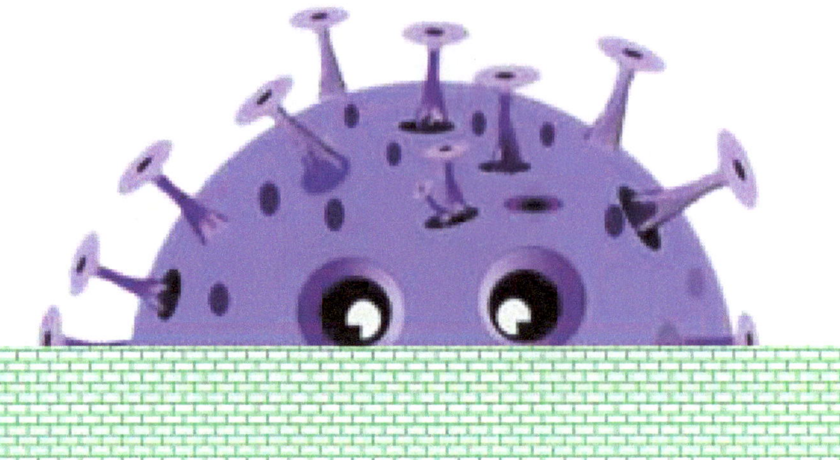

So where are they?

Can you guess where some
of them can be found?

In the ground, lakes, rivers, and seas.

They are also in the plants and trees.

In the air and in the breeze.

They get there when we cough or sneeze.

This is one way Covid and the flu get to you.

So how do we keep Vinny the Virus away?

Wash Your Hands

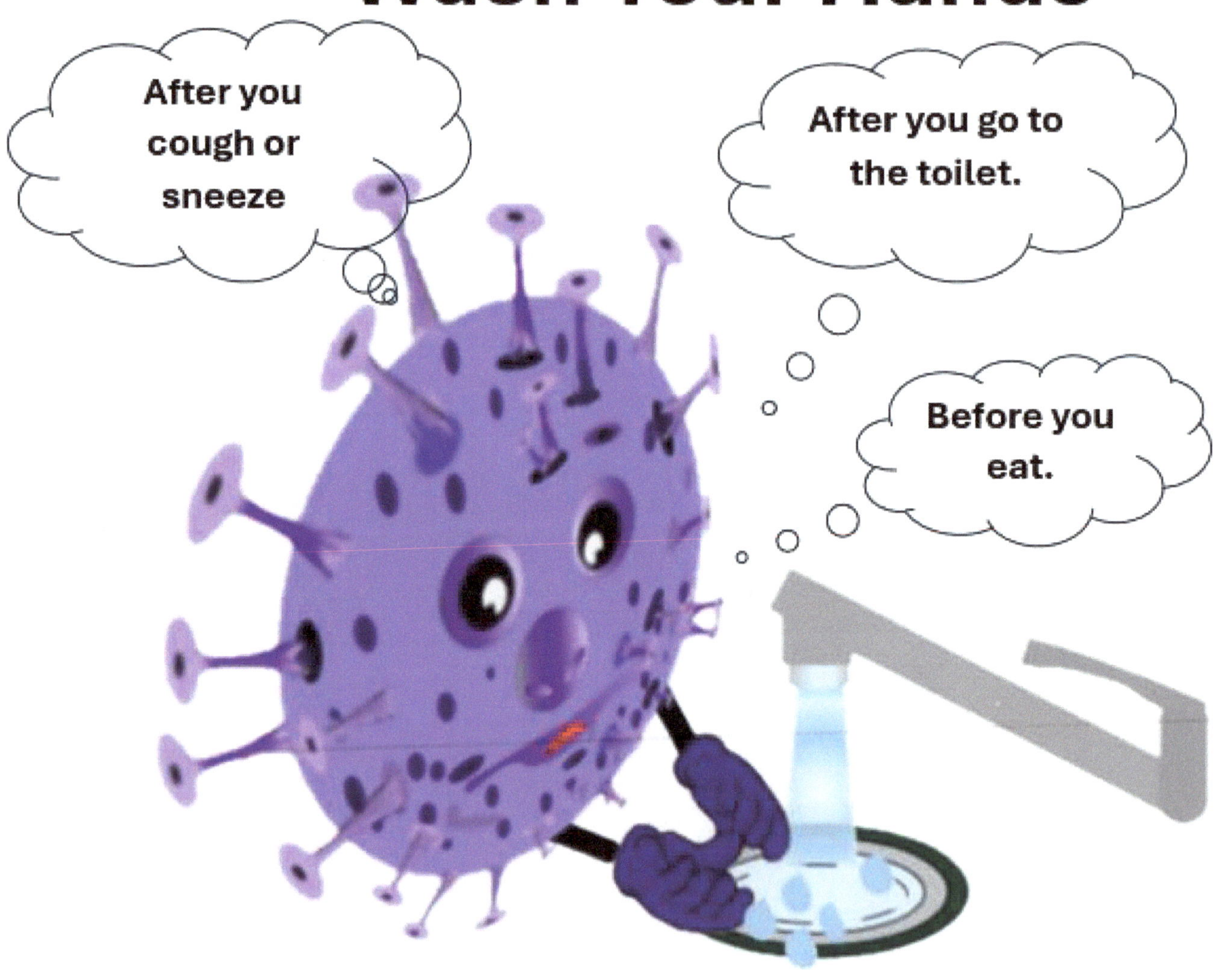

Cover your nose and mouth with a mask.

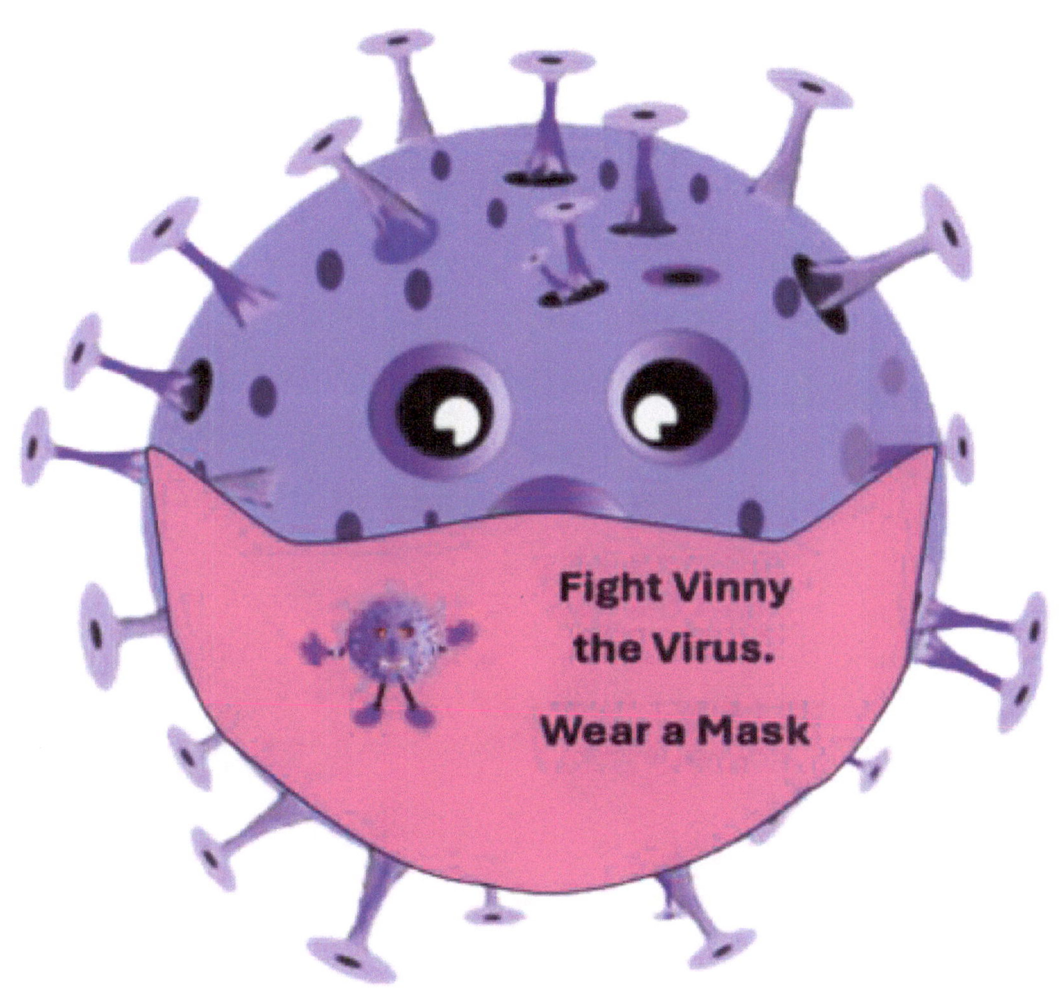

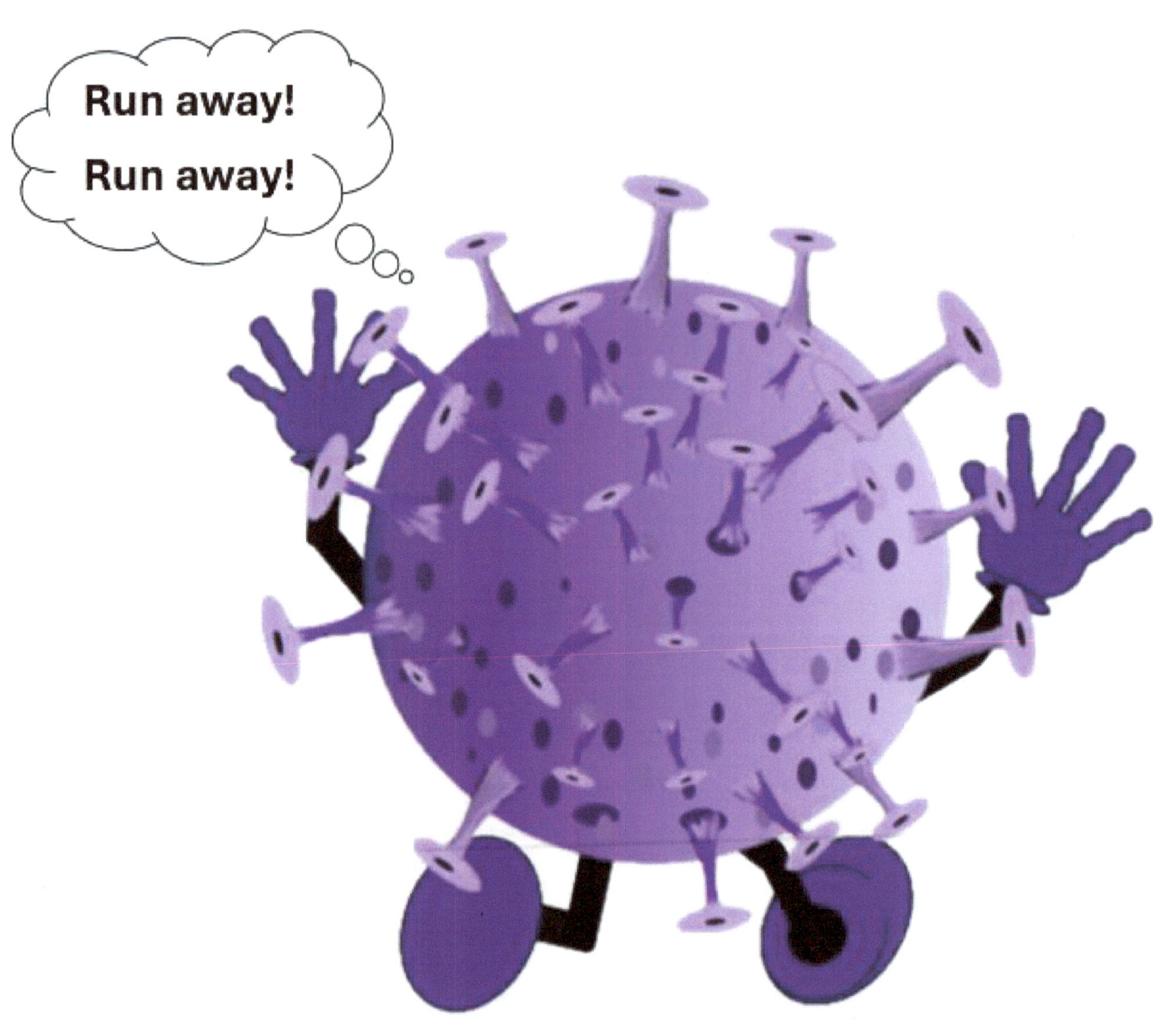

Some receive a vaccination.

If you need to cough or sneeze,
Use a tissue or use your sleeve.

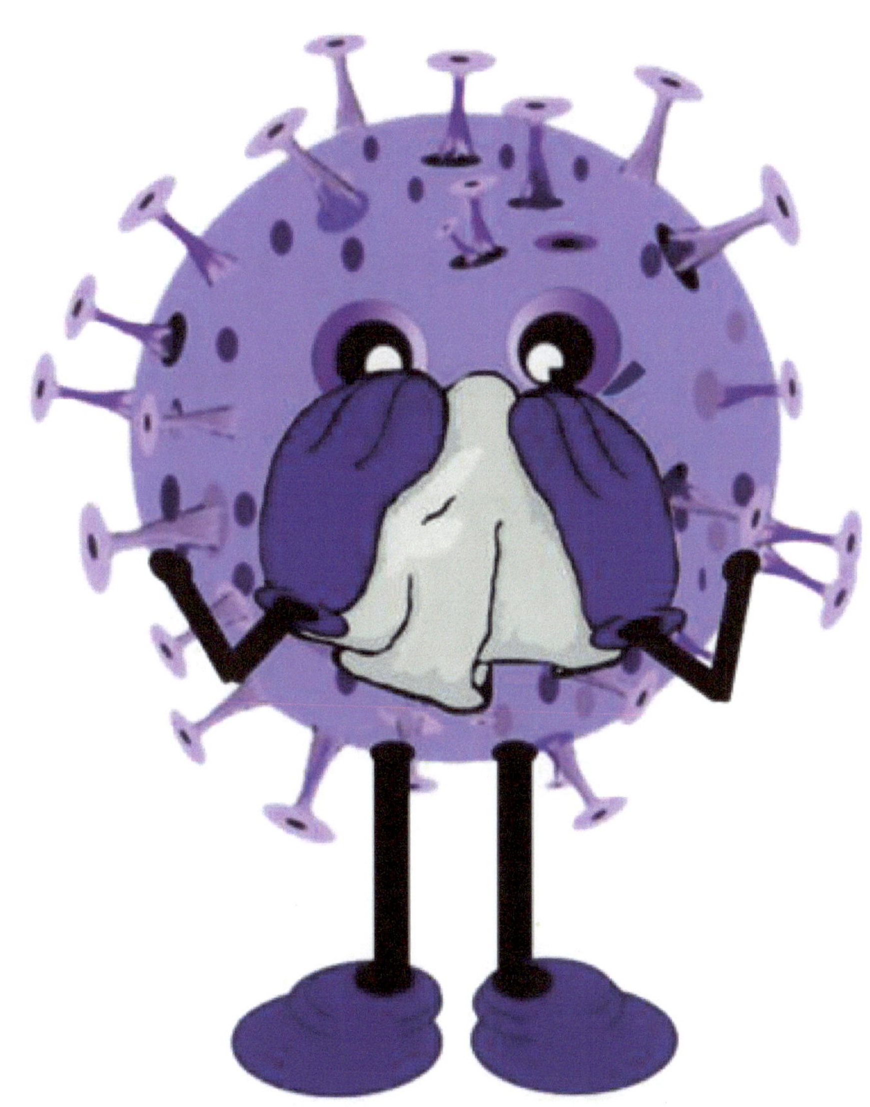

Don't be scared.

Don't be scared.

There are things you can do, to keep Vinny the Virus away from you.

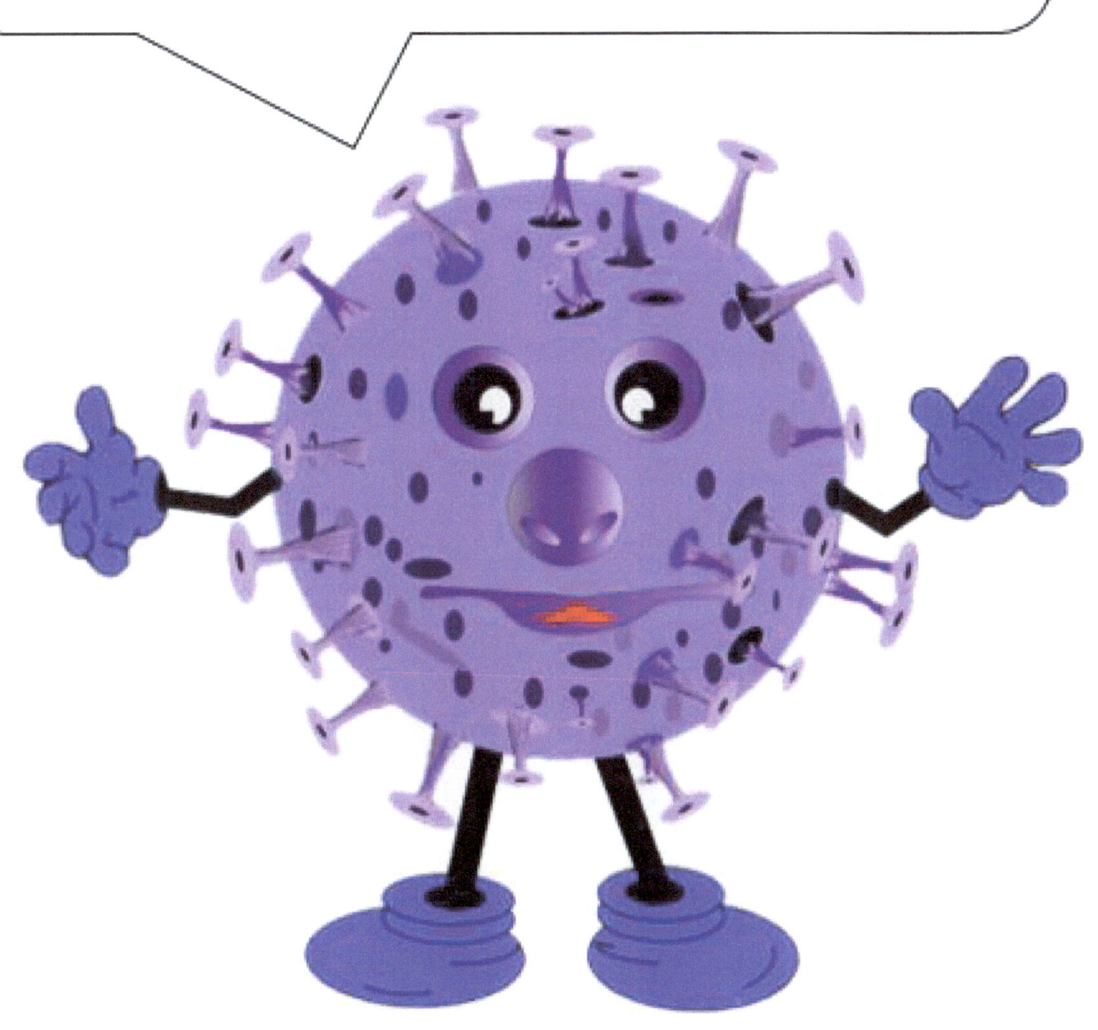

Now you know what to do to keep
Vinny the Virus away from you.

Fun Facts about Viruses

Fun Fact No: 1

Viruses are so tiny they cannot be seen with the naked eye or a normal microscope.

Fun Fact No: 2

They can only move around in moist environments such as the air, water, food and blood.

Fun Fact No: 3

Some viruses are beneficial by infecting and killing some bacteria. Some viruses have been used to treat cancer.

Fun Fact No: 4

Viruses cannot survive without a host. A host can be an animal, a human or a plant.

Fun Fact No: 5

Viruses do not need food. They do not eat or drink.